LURID CONFESSIONS

STEVE KOWIT

Carpenter Press

Acknowledgements:
Versions of these poems have appeared in *Amorotica; Antenna; Big Boulevard; The Brooklyn College Alumni Journal; Cafe Solo; Calafia; Cedar Rock; Citybender; Contact/II; Essence of Dragon Wings; For Neruda, For Chile; In Miss Virginia's Basement; Little Caesar; Maelstrom Review; Nausea; New Poetry (Australia); Pacific Poetry & Fiction Review; Poetry Now; Poets on Photography; Scholia Satyrica; Sree; The Second Coming; Vagabond; The Vagabond Anthology; Voices on the Last Frontier; Willmore City;* and in two previous collections: *Climbing the Walls* (Proexistence Press 1975), & *Cutting Our Losses* (Contact/II Press, 1982).

Published by:

CARPENTER PRESS ROUTE 4 POMEROY OHIO 45769

First Edition

LIBRARY OF CONGRESS CATALOGUING IN PUBLICATION DATA

Kowit, Steve
     Lurid confessions.

     I. Title
PS3561.087L8   1982   811'.54   82-12915

ISBN 0-914140-12-4

Cover drawing by Michael Previte
Frontispiece, "Young Madame Blavatsky," and photograph of the author by Mary Petrangelo Kowit

MEMBER
COSMEP
COMMITTEE OF SMALL MAGAZINE
EDITORS AND PUBLISHERS
BOX 703 SAN FRANCISCO. CA 94101

For Mary, for my parents, for my friends, for you.

Blue things are blue, red things are red . . .
That is what we call Paradise.
—*Amida Sutra*

I expect the angels to piss in my beer.
—*Henry Miller*

CONTENTS

1. climbing the walls

2. blue movies

3. trans-american express

4. home

1

Climbing the Walls

THE QUEUE

You have taken your place on what is surely
the longest line in the world,
longer by far than the ones at the movies
or at the motor vehicle bureau.
You dream, pick a speck
from your cuff, nibble your cuticle, hum
to yourself, flirt, scratch, argue—
anything to keep occupied.
How slowly it inches forward!
& then you think— how quickly it moves!
Look back— such a procession
of nostrils & hats! Now, instead of millions
ahead there are millions behind you.
The long, colorful queue of your fellow
creatures vanishes backward across the city
into the suburbs, over the prairie
& circles the globe. In front of you now
is only the fellow who crumples
to one knee, clutching his heart
& the woman whose head on the block
is screaming goodbye as the ax
whisks thru with a clean stroke.
Her glasses fall off.
The grapefruit that rolls to your feet
is her head.
You stumble forward at last, you
who thought your turn would never arrive,
your heart beating wildly at the tips
of your fingers like a blue ticket.

A VOTE FOR HAROLD

The kid who's taken the paper route for the summer,
a doughy, asthmatic schlemiel
with a blubbery bottom
& bifocals big as moondogs
& cockeyed hair
hasn't a shot at paperboy of the season
& two weeks in Miami.
For him a good day is passing the schoolyard
without getting punched in the head.
Our block is the worst. He has to pedal uphill
in the wind. You can hear him coming for miles,
straining & wheezing— then a forlorn
little squeal at the crest
like a possum shot from a tree
& a crash that rattles the dishes.
Then, after a silence, his broken,
woebegone voice among the azaleas.
I no longer lunge out of my chair like I used to,
but calmly stroll into the yard
& remove the handlebars from his thorax.
He blinks thickly, releasing a sob.
Together we salvage the home edition
that's scattered over the alley—
it too full of mayhem & ill luck:
an air disaster in Argentina,
a family of seven lost in a flood,
the hand of a refugee reaching thru barbed wire,
clutching at nothing, a hand so thin
it will eat anything— straw, dung, wind . . .
& then he is gone, wobbling into the gutter,
that exemplary herald of the Abyss
dogged on all sides
by curses & screeches & horns
& is lost in the distance
disheveled, & shaking his head
like a man who is forced to bear witness
to things too awful to mention,
& pedaling like hell.

CLIMBING THE WALLS

Fred, an apostate Jew, has accepted
Jesus Christ as his personal savior.

He runs down his bhakti-yoga in Denny's
over a pizza omelet & lemonade.

Bill's going back to the order;
Harry's in orgone therapy;

Alan's been in the Teaching 5 years.
& I too have no intention of circling

the stifling cage of my personal karma
forever. No indeed. I'm making my move

with a modest assortment of picks, drills,
jimmies, snips, saws, blasting

caps & a ladder made of my big &
little intestines knotted together.

MYSTERIES

Tonight, sick with the flu & alone, I drift
in confusion & neurasthenia surrendering
to the chaos & mystery of all things,
for tonight it comes to me like a sad but obvious revelation
that we know nothing at all.
Despite all our fine theories we don't have the foggiest
notion of why or how anything in this world exists
or what anything means or how anything fits
or what we or anyone else are doing here in the first place.
Tonight the whole business is simple beyond me.
Painfully I sit up in bed & look out the window
into the evening. There is a light on
in Marie's apartment. My neighbor Marie, the redhead,
is moving away. She found a cheaper apartment elsewhere.
She is packing up her belongings
The rest of the street is dark, bereft.
In this world, nothing is ruled out & nothing is certain.
A savage carnivorous primate bloated with arrogance
floating about on a tiny island
among the trillions of islands out in the darkness.
Did you know that the human brain was larger 40 millenia
    back?
Does that mean they were smarter?
It stands to reason they were but we simply don't know.
& what of the marriage dance of the scorpion?
Do whales breach from exuberance
or for some sort of navigational reason?
What does the ant queen know or do to provoke such
    undying devotion?
What of the coelacanth & the neapolina—
not a fossil trace for 300 million years
then one day there she is swimming around.
In the mangrove swamps the fruit-bats hang from the trees
& flutter their great black wings.
How does a turnip sprout from a seed?

Creatures that hatch out of eggs & walk about on the earth
as if of their own volition.
How does a leaf unwind on its stem & turn red in the fall
& drop like a feather onto the snowy fields of the spinning
    world?
What does the shaman whisper into the ear of the beetle
that the beetle repeats to the rain?
Why does the common moth so love the light
she is willing to die? Is it some incurable hunger for warmth?
At least that I can understand.
How & why does the salmon swim thousands of miles back
to find the precise streambed, the very rock
under which it was born? God knows what that urge is
to be home in one's bed if only to die. There have been dogs,
abandoned by families moving to other parts of the country
who have followed thru intricate cities,
over the wildest terrain— exhausted & bloody & limping—
a trail that in no way could be said to exist,
to scratch at a door it had never seen,
months, in cases, even years later.
Events such as these can not be explained. If indeed
we are made of the same stuff as seakelp & stars,
what that stuff is we haven't any idea.
The very atom eludes us.
Is it a myth & the cosmos an infinite series of Chinese boxes,
an onion of unending minusculation?
What would it look like apart from the grid of the language—
cut loose from its names—
Is there no solid ground upon which to plant our molecular
    flag?
What of the microorganic civilizations
living their complex domestic histories out in the roots of
    our hair?
Is there life in the stars?
Are there creatures like us weeping in furnished rooms
out past the solar winds in the incalculable dark
where everything's spinning away from everything else?
Are we just configurations of energy pulsing in space?

As if that explained this!
Is the universe conscious? Have we lived other lives?
Does the spirit exist? Is it immortal?
Do these questions even make sense?
& all this weighs on me like a verdict of exile.
I brush back the curtain an inch.
It flutters, as if by some ghostly hand.
Now Marie's light is off & the world is nothing again,
utterly vacant, sunyata, the indecipherable void. How
    awesome
& sad & mysterious everything is tonight.
Tell me this, was the Shroud of Turin really the deathshroud
    of Jesus?
What of those tears that gush from the wounds
of particular icons? Don't tell me they don't.
Thousands of people have seen them.
Did Therese Newman really survive on a wafer a day?
& the levitations of Eusapia Pallachino & St. Teresa.
& Salsky who suffered the stigmata in that old Victorian house
on Oak Street across from the Panhandle
on Good Friday. With my own eyes I saw them— his palms
    full of blood.
Where does everything disappear that I loved?
The old friends with whom I would wander about
lost in rhapsodic babble, stoned, in the dark:
Jim Fraser, Guarino, Steve Parker & Mednick & Burke—
squabbling & giggling over the cosmos. That walk-up
on 7th Street overlooking the tenement roofs of Manhattan.
Lovely Elizabeth dead & Ronnie OD'd on a rooftop in
    Brooklyn
& Jerry killed in the war & the women— those dark,
furtive kisses & sighs; all the mysterious moanings of sex.
Where did I lose the addresses of all those people I knew?
Now even their names are gone: taken, lost, abandoned,
vanished into the blue. Where is the OED
I won at Brooklyn College for writing a poem
& the poem itself decades gone & the black & gold Madison
High School tennis team captain's jacket I was so proud of.
Where is that beaded headband? The marvelous Indian flute?

That book of luminous magic-marker paintings Eliot did?
& where is Eliot now? & Greg Marquez? & Marvin Torfield?
Where are the folding scissors from Avenida Abancay in Lima?
Where is the antique pocket watch Rosalind Eichenstein gave
     me—
I loved it so— the painted shepherd playing the flute
in the greenest, most minuscule hills.
I bet some junkie on 7th Street took it
but there's no way now to find out. It just disappeared
& no one & nothing that's lost will ever be back.
How came a cuneiform tablet unearthed by the Susquehanna?
Why was Knossos never rebuilt?
What blast flattened the Tunguska forest in 1908?
& those things that fall from the sky— manna
from heaven & toads & huge blocks of ice & alabaster
& odd-shaped gelatinous matter— fafrotskis
of every description & type
that at one time or another have fallen out of the sky.
The alleged Venezuelan fafrotski— what is it exactly
& where did it come from?
& quarks & quasars & black holes . . . The woolly mammoth,
one moment peacefully grazing on clover in sunlight,
an instant later quick-frozen into the arctic
antediluvian north. What inconceivable cataclysm occurred?
How did it happen?
What would my own children have looked like?
Why is there always one shoe on the freeway?
Why am I shivering? What am I even doing
writing this poem? Is it all nothing but ego— my name
screaming out from the grave?
I look out the window again. How strange,
now the tobacco shop on the corner is lit.
A gaunt, mustachioed figure steps to the doorway & looks at
     my window
& waves. Why, it's Fernando Pessoa!
I wave back— Fernando! Fernando! I cry out.
But he doesn't see me. He can't. The light snaps off.
The tobacco shop disappears into the blackness,
        into the past . . .

Who was the ghost in the red cape who told Henry IV he
    would die?
What of those children raised by wolves & gazelles?
What of spontaneous human combustion— those people
who burst into flame? Is space really curved?
Did the universe have a beginning
or did some sort of primal matter always exist?
Either way it doesn't make sense!
How does the pion come tumbling out of the void
& where does it vanish once it is gone?
& we too— into what & where do we vanish?
For the worms, surely we too are meat on the hoof.
Frankly it scares me, it scares the hell out of me.
The back of my neck is dripping with sweat . . . a man
with a fever located somewhere along the Pacific Coast
in the latter half of the 20th century by the Julian calendar:
a conscious, momentary configuration; a bubble in the stew,
a child of the dark. I am going to stand up now if I can,
—that's what I'm going to do,
& make my way to the kitchen
& find the medicine Mary told me was there.
Perhaps she was right. Perhaps it will help me to sleep.
Yes, that's what I'll do— I'll sleep & forget.
We know only the first words of the message— if that.
I could weep when I think of how lovely it was
in its silver case all engraved with some sort of floral design,
the antique watch that Rosalind gave me years ago
on the lower east side of Manhattan
when we were young & in love & had nothing but time—
    that watch
with its little shepherd playing a flute on the tiny hillside,
gone now like everything else.
Where in the name of Christ did it disappear to—
that's what I want to know!

IN THE DARK

blah blah

—old proverb

I'd meant
to watch
the sunset
but got
talking
to this guy
about
Gurdjieff
& don Juan
& forgot
why I'd come:
on & on
about
don Juan
& Gurdjieff
& illumination.

DESPERATE SOLUTIONS

For weeks now the parts of a poem,
a scramble of fittings & rivets & gears,
have been clanking around in your head
like the guts of an unassembled machine,
till at last,
with one jolting image,
a gift,
the device you had never been able to find,
everything snaps into place
& you dive for your notebook—
But jesus, there's never a pen
when you need one:
the scripto blotches,
the pentel's a leaker,
the flair scrapes like a bone.
In your bottom drawer is a magic marker
that hasn't worked in a decade,
the stub of a pencil,
an orange crayola,
& 12 thousand paperclips & erasers.
& digging around in a box on the floor
you karate your head
on the underside of the table
& everything crashes about you
including the coffee.
It spills down your t-shirt.
You shriek
as your flesh starts to blister
& that's it!
That's all you'll take!
So you hurl the mug at the wall
& snatching a pin from its cushion
you jab it as deep as she'll go
into the tip of your finger.

Then biting your tongue & spitting in pain
you goose it once with your thumb
till a sleek jet spurts from the wound
to the page
like a leak sprung in a hose
or the blow of the tiniest whale,
only red.
There! Perfect!
As ever, the poem,
which began as a simple machine,
has turned itself into another rube goldberg
contraption— a slapstick improvisation
born out of chaos,
plucked from disaster,
& written in blood.

LETTER TO DEAN PICKER

Dear Robert D. Picker, you've done me a turn
by telling me whom I've next to pursue
in order to get what I thought I had earned
but apparently not as I haven't yet learned
the King's English according to you—
& it's true O Acting Associate Dean:
my style's atrocious, abrupt, full of spleen,
unruly, contentious, uncalled-for— in short,
while paying perfunctory court to the king
I pinch the queen's rump & tickle her knee
& pretty much say what I bloody well mean.

But with or without another degree
I've learned a thing or two or three—
how to fashion a poem that'll curdle your sauce,
how to ride a dean as well as a horse
(metaphorically speaking that is of course)
& I've only to wait till the next full moon
then *academus fatuous! Squatonabroom!*
find me a moosetail, eat a bean,
& puff! no more Acting Associate Dean.

HATE MAIL

I got a letter from an old acquaintance in New York
asking me to send some of my prose poems
to her literary magazine, *Unhinged*.
I should have known better.
In the old days she'd fluttered about
the coffee houses baring her long teeth.
We'd smile up politely & cover our throats.
But time makes you forget & ambition got the better of me
& a week later I got my poems back with a terse note:
Sorry, but this third-rate pornographic crap isn't for us.
& may I point out it is presumptuous of you
not to have enclosed a self-addressed stamped envelope.
Just who in hell does little Stevie Kowit think he is?
I was nonplussed.
I sent a stamp back with a note explaining
that I hadn't thought I was submitting to her magazine
so much as answering her letter.
I received a blistering reply:
Who was I kidding? What I had sent was a submission
to *Unhinged*, pure & simple.
In passing she referred to me as juvenile,
adolescent, immature, a sniveling brat, an infant
& a little baby—
truly the letter of a raving lunatic.
I suppose it would have been best to have ignored it,
forgot the whole thing,
but that little Stevie Kowit business started eating at me
so I dropped a one-liner in an envelope & sent it off:
Dear C, you are a ca-ca pee-pee head.

THANK YOU

The big creative writing gig
at the university
turned out to be one section
of freshman comp,
but when you're hungry
even the crumbs are a *mitzvah*.
"Thanks very much—"
& I meant it,
but I suddenly felt smaller
& when I looked up
all I could see
was the underside of his desk.
The windows had shot out of reach.
"You're sure you can handle it now?"
"Oh yes, I'm certain!"
I grinned up at his knee.
My tongue slipped out.
My coccyx started to twitch.
(Did he really
bend over & scratch
me behind the ear?!)
                    "& you say
you don't mind coming in
for just one section now?"
"Oh God no! That's just perfect!"
My voice
a squeak from the floorboards.
What was left of me
stared up from under his wingtips.
One tap I was done for.
There was no time to waste.

I scurried for a crack
under the door
like a cockroach caught in the light.
But I was still a little too big.
"Well thanks, thanks very much!"
There, that did it!
A germ
sneezed out of somebody's nostril
has never moved quicker.

LYCANTHROPY IN SOUTH PASADENA

When they drag out the latest books & awards
I fly into a rage
& leap to my feet
& before they can stop me
I'm tearing into the poets!
All talon & fang
I mangle them good & proper,
ripping out throats
& wrenching off limbs at the sockets,
intestines & eyeballs
flying in every direction.
My companions,
critics themselves,
but taken aback nonetheless,
suddenly remember long-standing appointments
& head for the street.
Grunting & heaving,
I stumble into the fog,
moon at my back like a smudge
& blood on my tongue,
till at last,
with a final hideous shriek
I drop to my knees
& sink to the ground
staring into the dark
where the pale hub of the moon
wheels thru the clouds.
God knows how long I remain there
till ever so slowly
the twisted fist of my breathing
unclenches & calms.
The talons retract.
The canines slip back into my gums
& I come to myself
just as the first ray of light
burns off the last of the mist.

A leaf or two falls.
Citizen, scour these woods as you will
with your blazing torch,
that fiend is gone!
By midafternoon, clean shaven
& dressed, like everyone else,
in a jacket & tie,
I pass thru the peaceable streets
of the kingdom
as one of your own.

CREDO

I am of those who believe
different things on different days.

2

Blue Movies

IT WAS YOUR SONG

I saw her once, briefly,
in the park
among the folk musicians
twenty years ago—
a barefoot child of twelve
or thirteen
in a light serape
& the faded, skintight levis
of the era. I recall
exactly how she stood there
one foot on the rise
of the fountain
finger-picking that guitar
& singing
in the most alluring
& delicious voice,
& as she sang she'd
flick her hair
behind one shoulder
in a gesture that meant nothing,
yet I stood there
stunned.
One of those exquisite
creatures of the Village
who would hang around
Rienzi's & Folk City,
haunting all the coffee houses
of MacDougal Street,
that child
has haunted my life
for twenty years.
Forgive me.
I am myself reticent
to speak of it,
this embarrassing infatuation

for a young girl,
seen once, briefly,
decades back,
as I hurried thru the park.
But there it is.
& I have written this
that I might linger at her side
a moment longer,
& to praise the Alexandrian,
Cavafy, that devotee
of beautiful boys,
& shameless rhapsodist
of the ephemeral encounter.
Cavafy, it was your song
from which I borrowed
both the manner & the courage.

A SWELL IDEA

One of these days
while demonstrating the use
of the possessive pronoun
preceding the gerund
I'll tell her a little joke,
grow playful,
stroke the soft hairs
on the back of Melanie's neck
then slip my hand
over her breast.
Just as I've dreamed!
She'll groan.
She'll giggle & put
her hand over mine.
She'll love it!
If not, what have I lost?
If she screams
& the others rush in
I'll deny everything.
I'll stand there
shaking my head,
"She's crazy she's
making it up she
practically forced me
for chrissake I'm
sick I'm a sick man
I need help
Help me!"
I'll cry out
in a hoarse,
broken voice
& slip to my knees
& bury my face in my hands.

THE CREEP

The creep moves in on strange women.
"Harold," he says.
"How ya doin' tonight?"

You clutch your purse.
Turn down what street you will,
he is beside you,

leaning in— the open lace
of an enormous sneaker
slapping against your ankle

like long, loose arms.

AMABO, MEA DULCIS IPSITHILLA

Ipsithilla, say the word
I'll be at your door in a flash.
But for chrissake
don't change your mind
at the last minute
like last time
& lock me out
with a cock & bull story
about another appointment.
Just be there
in black nylons
or wearing the nightgown
I bought you or
nothing,
nothing at all—
simply anointed
& waiting
& please
make it quick—
the thing is growing enormous.

WANTED— SENSUOUS WOMAN WHO CAN HANDLE 12 INCHES OF MAN

from an ad in the Miami Phoenix

She was sensuous to a fault
& perfectly willing
tho somewhat taken aback.
In fact, at first,
she noticed no one at the door at all.
"Down here! . . . down here! . . ."
I shrieked.
—Need I add that once again
I left unsatisfied.

RENEWAL

One of those lubricious teenage latin beauties,
a sloe-eyed fox
with a small cross like a grave
between her breasts
gave up her seat on the S bus,
oozed thru the mob,
& began rubbing it off against my leg.
& not discreetly, either—
she absolutely abandoned herself!
I stared straight ahead,
afraid to move,
hardly believing it,
but managed, nevertheless,
to work my free hand
down to where I felt it
would do us both the most good.
The girl went crazy.
We both did.
We must have blazed away for 40 minutes,
all the way to 16th & Biscayne.
I got home hours later,
shaken but whistling—
like a man whose life has been renewed
by a miracle:
an ineradicable smirk on my face
& above my head
a halo clanging like a trash can lid.

MILLIE

On weekdays, Bert, a beefy roofer
with clown-sized feet & a boozer's gut
is as quiet a neighbor as I've ever had.
But Friday evenings he trucks home
with two cases of Coors
& by Saturday night
You can hear the cookware flying:
                    "You goddam lying
son of a fucking shit!"
It's Millie, his old lady.
Retiring as Penelope sober, drunk
she's a double medusa— all mayhem & lungs.
It's absolute carnage.
The duplex trembles.
We clutch the arms of our chairs
like whitewater canoers. Nobody sleeps.
At first when they moved in
I figured her for an aging waitress at Hojos
but one afternoon all chummy & flushed,
she confided that she was an RN
for terminal cases:
                    "Steven, it's awful.
You roll them over & clean up their mess
& pray they don't terminate
on your shift.
Mostly they just lie there & moan
& there's nothing anybody can do."
Wrong, Millie.
You could show up polluted & shrieking.
Kick over their IV's.
Fling their bedpans around.
Smithereen their precious crockery against the walls
until they can't stop trembling.

Rattle them up good
the way you rattle up this neighborhood
when you are in your cups
& maniacal.
Let them die without the least regret:
after you, oblivion could only be a blessing.

KOWIT

Sometimes when I'm not there to defend myself
the friends start playing *Kowit*.
Right from the start, the game,
begun with what seemed nothing
if not innocent affection,
takes a nasty turn:
from quietly amused to openly derisive,
ruthless, scathing, & at last
maniacally sadistic—
a psychopathic bacchanal of innuendo,
malice & vindictive lies.
It's jealousy & spite is what it is of course.
They're rankled by my talent & integrity,
the editors & fancy women who surround me.
So Kowit's torn upon the rack
& barbecued alive
& chewed out of his skin like a salami
till there is nothing left of him
but blood & phlegm & scat
& fingernails & teeth
& the famous Kowit penis
which is passed about the room
to little squeals of laughter
like a ridiculous hat.

LURID CONFESSIONS

One fine morning they move in for the pinch
& snap on the cuffs— just like that.
Turns out they've known all about you for years,
have a file the length of a paddy-wagon
with everything— tapes, prints, film . . .
the whole shmear. Don't ask me how but
they've managed to plug a mike into one of your molars
& know every felonious move & transgression
back to the very beginning, with ektachromes
of your least indiscretion & peccadillo.
Needless to say, you are thrilled,
tho sitting there in the docket
you bogart it, tough as an old tooth—
your jaw set, your sleeves rolled
& three days of stubble . . . Only,
when they play it back it looks different:
a life common & loathsome as gum stuck to a chair.
Tedious hours of you picking your nose,
scratching, eating, clipping your toenails . . .
Alone, you look stupid; in public, your rapier
wit is slimy & limp as an old bandaid.
They have thousands of pictures of people around you
stifling yawns. As for sex— a bit
of pathetic groping among the unlovely & luckless:
a dance with everyone making steamy love in the dark
& you alone in a corner eating a pretzel.
You leap to your feet protesting
that's not how it was, they have it all wrong.
But nobody hears you. The bailiff
is snoring, the judge is cleaning his teeth,
the jurors are all wearing glasses with eyes painted open.
The flies have folded their wings & stopped buzzing.

In the end, after huge doses of coffee,
the jury is polled. One after another
they manage to rise to their feet
like narcoleptics in August, sealing your fate:
Innocent ... innocent ... innocent ... Right down the line.
You are carried out screaming.

THE POETRY READING WAS A DISASTER

& I had expected so much.
All the big kahunas would be there—
the New York literati & foundation honchos
& publishing magi & hordes of insouciant groupies
& millions of poets—
the shaggy vanguard in green adidas snapping their fingers,
surrealists whirling about by the ceiling
like adipose St. Teresas in mufti,
Bolinas cowboys & tatterdemalion beatniks
& Buddhists with mandarin beards & big goofy eyes
& Iowa poets in blazers & beanies
& Poundians nodding gigantic foreheads.
What tumultuous applause would erupt when I stepped
to the stage. What a thunder of adoration!
The room would be shaking.
The very city would tremble.
The whole damn Pacific Plate start to shudder.
One good jolt & everything west of the San Andreas
would squirt back into Mesopotamian waters
& this time for good—
jesus but they would love me!
. . . Except when I got to the place it was tiny,
a hole in the wall,
& only a handful had shown up
& as soon as I walked to the front of the room
a kid started whining,
a chap in the second row fell asleep
& a trashed-out punk rocker with a swastika t-shirt,
drool on his chin & arms down to his knees
started cackling out loud. The razor blade
chained at his throat bounced up & down.
Somewhere a couple must have been screwing around
under their seats— I heard tongues
lapping it up, orgasmic weeping,
groans that grew louder and louder.
The kid wouldn't shut up.

The sleeper started to snore.
Potato chip eaters in every direction
were groping around in tinfoil bags
while the poetry lover, my host,
was oohing & aahing in all the wrong places.
I looked up politely. Couldn't they please,
please be a little more quiet.
Somebody snickered. There was a slap &
the brat started to bawl.
Someone stormed out in a huff slamming the door.
Another screamed that I was a pig & a sexist.
A heavy-set lady in thick mensa glasses leaped to her feet
& announced that she was a student of Mark Strand.
In the back, the goon with the tattooed shirt
& the blade was guffawing & flapping his wings.
What could I do?
I read for all I was worth, straight from the heart,
all *duende* & dazzle—
no one & nothing was going to stop me!
Inspired at last, I read to a room
that had fallen utterly silent.
They must have been awed.
I wailed to the winds like Cassandra,
shoring our language against the gathering dark.
I raged at the heavens themselves
& ended the last set in tears, on my knees. . . .
When I looked up it was night & I was alone
except for an old lady up on a stepladder
scrubbing what looked like glops of shit off the wall
& humming.
The place stank of ammonia.
Thank you so much
had been scribbled over my briefcase in lipstick
or blood. Someone had stepped on my glasses,
lifted my wallet,
& sliced off all of my buttons,
half of my mustache,
& one of my balls.

BLUE MOVIES

You loll in bed,
your head full of blue movies—
a roll in the hay with your leggy starlets,
reviews of your magnum opus,
scenes from your life in the jungles
with Camilo Torres—
yourself the charismatic troubadour
shaman stud guerrilla savant.
You doorknob! You clock
pretending to be a timebomb!
Your wife kisses you,
the birds sing,
the sun streams thru the blinds.
While you tug at your covers & dream,
the provident roaches
at work in the cracks of the cupboard
are stocking their shelves,
& the little ants in the weeds
are building their civilizations.

3

Trans-American Express

THE NOVIOS

I spent the whole day packing books away into cartons—
hundreds of quarterly magazines & collections of verse
filled for the most part with slush—
mannered, grandiloquent drivel:
page after page of obtuse & tedious pigshit.
Next Tuesday I'll take them down to the post office
& that will be that. I'll be rid of the whole lot.
We'll fly into Mexico City as light & unencumbered as birds.
First thing, I'll walk up Avenida Juarez
& buy a *torta de queso* & a *licuado*,
then stroll thru the Alameda,
that park with the scarlet shoeshine stands
& magnificent tile benches
& all the young lovers, the *novios*,
sitting under the trees
popping each other's pimples.
I happen to know at the far end of the Alameda
there's a bookstore a block long
where for 60 pesos
I can pick up a nice fat collection of poems by Nicanor Parra.

LA RESOLANA

Good bread & strong
weed. No stars
up but a smudge
of moon
thru the clouds.
In the dark a
scrawny Mexican dog
wanders about the camp
searching for scraps.
brother . . . brother . . .
he yelps out
with that sad
touching love
dogs have for us.
& it's true, I
recognize him
at once. I rise,
tuck her sleeping bag
about Mary's throat,
set a small meal
at his feet,
& slide back into
my hammock.
The clouds unravel.
The moon rolls out
like a coin
released from a fist.

XOCHICALCO

This morning, up at those ruins
gleaming like tombs in the sun,
the three of us sat in the shade
of a crumbling temple
& considered the seasons.
We modeled out the ecliptic with stones
fumbling like grade school kids
with equations we only half understood
& giggled over our ignorance,
there where a thousand years ago
Toltec astronomers
calculated the revolutions of Venus
& perfected the calendar.
Xochi-calco: beflowered city. Rolando
called it a geophysical center
where priests engaged in a study of time itself
& Topiltzin, the prince, revealed
himself as the feathered serpent.
Gold, blood & cerulean flowers
flourished among the wild grass.
Up there you could see the whole countryside:
the road unwinding into the valley
under a sky of pure ceremonial blue.
It was our last day here before heading south.
In the afternoon,
we wandered among the temples,
strolled thru the ball court,
offered the last of our bread
to a couple of scrawny dogs,
& tried our hand at some rubbings
that ended up like those scribbles
people make in rapture, under acid,
imagining they've caught some unspeakable essence.
Too bad.
I would have wished to have taken with me

a print of that signature
Mary discovered in midafternoon,
half buried among the priests & glyphs
on the Temple of Quetzalcoatl:
an exquisite hand
pulling a block of worked stone
by a braided rope—
one of those fragments the rains
of a thousand years had not yet laid waste.
I was shaken by it,
it was so tender & deftly wrought
& spoke so poignantly of the artist's life
that I lie here, a millenium later,
awakened by it to a storm of feelings,
reminded of all these people I won't see again,
& of my own life, the greater
part of which is already spent.
& of my own work.
Tomorrow we leave.
Our backpacks lie by the open window.
Out over the canyon
Venus-Xolotl drifts thru the night sky.
The clock ticks like a restive heart.
With love & sorrow
I have carved these figures out of the language
that you may remember:
Julia . . . Rolando . . . Miguel . . .
called forth,
your faces drift thru the dark like spirits.

LA MUJER

I was resting in the shadows of a ruined temple
up at Monte Alban
when a man who had been slicing back the weeds
with his machete offered me a woman.
He wanted 40 bucks for her. I laughed
at him & said —in fractured Spanish—
40 dollars was outrageous.
That I wouldn't pay it.
That I wasn't just some stupid gringo.
He shook his head, all innocence, & raised
one palm up in a merchant's vow—
"Genuino . . . genuino . . ."
& with the other held her out for me to look at.
"Muy bonita!" he said gravely.
& she was. She was beautiful. Seated,
with her hands curled at her knees,
a gray stone figure in a beaded headband
& bracelets, all covered with the yellow
clay of the high desert.
He himself was Zapotec I guess
or a mestizo— small & delicate
& with a little Chaplin mustache
& an old sombrero
& *huaraches*,
& pants rolled half-way to his knees— trousers
the color of nothing anymore,
a faded blue dusted with gold
like that country . . .
In Mexico, replicas like those are everywhere
& I suppose I could have found one just as fine
among the black flutes of the Oaxaca market,
or at Sanborn's in the city.
But this was half his living, & besides,
up there, in the shadows of that temple,
under that sky . . .

So we dickered for a while until we struck
a bargain: 40
pesos & an old sweater
& I took her from him.
"*Muy barato*," he whispered
with a mournful headshake,
but he was well pleased. & I too,
I too! —As much for the occasion
as the woman. Monte Alban
in the hills above Oaxaca
where a campesino offered me a woman:
genuino . . . muy bonita . . . muy barato . . .

CUTTING OUR LOSSES

In a downtown San Jose hotel,
exhausted & uptight & almost broke,
we blew 16 *colones* & got stewed on rum.
You lounged in bed
reading *Hermelinda Linda* comics
while I stumbled drunk around the room
complaining
& reciting poems out of an old anthology.
I read that Easter elegy of Yeats'
which moved you,
bringing back that friend of yours,
Bob Fishman, who was dead.
You wept. I felt terrible.
We killed the bottle, made a blithered
kind of love & fell asleep.
Out in the Costa Rican night
the weasels of the dark held a fiesta
celebrating our safe arrival in their city
& our sound sleep.
We found our Ford Econoline next
morning where we'd left it,
on a side street, but ripped
apart like a piñata,
like a tortured bird, wing
window busted in, a door
sprung open on its pins like an astonished beak.
Beloved, everything we lost— our old blues
tapes, the telephoto lens, the Mayan priest,
that ancient Royal Portable I loved,
awoke me to how tentative & delicate
& brief & precious it all is, & was
for that a sort of aphrodisiac— tho bitter
to swallow. That evening,

drunk on loss, I loved you
wildly, with a crazy passion, knowing
as I did, at last, the secret
of your own quietly voluptuous heart— you
who have loved always with a desperation
born as much of sorrow as of lust,
being, I suppose, at once unluckier,
& that much wiser to begin with.

THE GARDEN

Years ago we owned two cats who hated each other.
When I said we had better give one away
you wouldn't hear of it— you
were adamant, outraged . . .
relenting only weeks later when it was clear
they were going to tear each other to shreds.
I remember the speech you made:
if it came to that we would give away Sluggo,
our loveable calico,
who could purr his way into anyone's heart.
For in less tolerant hands, Mphahlele,
our difficult, misanthropic gray
might be abused, or abandoned . . . or worse— whereas
if he lived with us he would be loved always.
& of course you were right,
tho God knows you have paid dearly
for a compassion as absolute
& unyielding
as the copper sheet of the Mexican sky
rising each morning over that house
high in the hills of Chiapas
that you loved so
with its eleven rooms,
those great hanging bells of datura,
that courtyard, tangle
of wild vines
that you would never let me weed
to begin a garden,
insisting in that quiet way of yours
that every creature
had as much right to live as we had,
& that it was a garden.

SMALL BOATS

The California tuna fisherman
who bought my van in Puntarenas
had a son who'd been killed in the war.
I remember sitting in the heat & listening.
He was a bald guy with a bulbous nose,
& a talker. He made his
wife bring in Mike's photo.
Then he started in on the Chinese,
how they were going to take over the world.
"William, don't . . . please . . .
no one's interested . . ."
The coffee cup rattled in her fingers.
Afterwards we bussed back along the coast road,
a thick fog rolling in off the Pacific
like a Sung scroll:
small boats
disappearing in the mist.

THEY ARE LOOKING FOR CHE GUEVARA

The lecturer writes the phrase *free enterprise* on the board in
    green chalk.
Above it white pustular fissures appear, which is the strangler
fig taking root in that part of the map devoted to Indonesia.
The metallic pit of the fruit grown from the miracle seed of the
    green revolution begins ticking.
The peasants dig in. The secret bombing begins.
The porpoise & bison & whooping crane lie down on top of
    the lecturer's desk & begin disappearing.
Meanwhile the Huns push on to the Yalu River
searching for Che Guevara.
The CIA is hunting for him in the Bolivian Andes.
Ferdinand Marcos & 6,000 Green Berets are hunting for him in
    the Philippines.
Ian Smith is hunting him down in Zimbabwe.
A small flame appears in the map of Asia:
it is that part they have burnt down searching for Che Guevara,
    queen-bee of the revolution.
They are hunting for him in Angola, Korea, Guatemala, the
    Congo, Brazil, Iran, Greece, Lebanon, Chile.
9,000 Ozymandian paratroops drop over Santo Domingo with
    searchlights, searching for him.
He is not there. He is gone. He is hiding among the Seminoles.
He throws the knife into the treaty with Osceola.
He conspires with Denmark Vesey.
In Port-au-Prince he is with Toussaint.
He reappears later at Harper's Ferry.
He is in Nicaragua, in Cuba where they have embargoed the
    rain.
The CIA has traced him to Berkeley, but he is in Algeria too
& Uruguay, Spain, Portugal, Guam, Puerto Rico.
Not all the ears of the dead of Asia will lead them to him.
He goes home, embraces his wife, embraces Hildita, embraces
    the children of Buenos Aires,

50

gives his compadre Fidel an *abrazo*, lights his pipe,
pours a cup of *maté*, takes a pill for his asthma,
cleans his rifle, reloads it, writes the First Declaration of
   Havana.
Torpedoes of Intergalactic Capital, Inc. blow up the screaming
   hair of the global village.
B52s drone overhead. It is dawn. They are checking every
   frontier. They are looking for Che Guevara.

"NERUDA'S REMAINS WERE EXPELLED THIS WEEK . . ."

In a pitch of bone it is singing at night
from its Andean crypt its rhapsodic,
implacable hymns to the people, its loves
& a lamentation that rumbles up from the pit
of the land like a temblor of music
entwined in the roots of the corn.
Wherever they plant his corpse
they harvest his voice.

On the coast, in the smothering beat
of its surf its insistent note:
the disenfranchised fish & inland
the Araucanian tilling the broken stone:
even the fat caciques of the corporate state
with their medallions & rings & executions
have heard the news that whistles up
from the bones where they hum
in a subterranean wind.

—Get rid of it! Get rid of that thing!
that vagabond corpse haunting the land
with its singing seductive heart
like a spreading stream!

                       But they can't.
Pieces lie scattered over the uplands,
fixed in the rock at Chuquicamata,
the loom of the fields; bits
have been washed in the crystalline falls.
The puma has known him at night
amid the dark leaves;
he is in the grain of the coast;
he has mingled his blood with the loam;
he has seeded it all; in every apple
you suck, he is singing!

*—Dig it up! Root it out! Get rid of that voice
with its wallowing freedoms!*

They would have the lights of the hazelnut tree
go out over Chile.
But they can't. They can't do a thing.
He remains where he's been
& there isn't a foot of the landscape he isn't.

Over the narrow tomb of the nation
the hair of his luminous grave is sprouting,
a perdurable swordlike agave,
from the center of which a heart
more red than the fresh rose of blood,
louder than flashing copper
& glowing like dawn
uprises
& blooms
& is singing.

TRANS-AMERICAN EXPRESS

Regaling us with stories
of her epic bus excursion
from the west coast to Manhattan,
Pat, the O.B. go-go dancer,
mentioned that a pal of hers from Reno,
earned a living one lean season
giving head
on the back seat
of the cross-country Greyhound.
It got me thinking
of all those second class Mexican buses,
the ones that were decked out like altars
with fringe-festooned windows
& plastic flowers
& votive candles
& the Virgin of Guadalupe
over the brilliantined head of the driver
& how we would hurtle over
precipitous backwater roads
to end in those sleepy towns
full of jacarandas & dust:
a burro in shade by a wall,
the vultures wheeling above us,
invisible Indian women with infants
begging in doorways,
kids with yellow boxes of chiclets
walking the streets all afternoon
for twenty centavos.
—That Pichucalco run, remember?
Quetzaltenango, where we froze all night.
Dusk on that white washboard road
in Quintana Roo:
hunters drifting like wraiths
thru the mist.
Laconic *chicleros*
insisting we take their seats to stay dry

in the teeming Peten
on that bus with the busted windows
Tikal— the ruins of white temples
in the jungle— monkeys
howling in the trees,
incredible starlight & rain
& then to get stranded
crossing the Rio Dulce back—
sixteen hours of stolid mestizos
with bracelets of chickens.
& south over the Andes— the bus
to Tumaco, Riobamba, Pomasqui,
Huancayo to Cuzco. . . .
& once, in that Andean vast,
before dawn, in Peru,
on the *altiplano*, in moonlight,
plowing our way thru the dust,
a herd of vicuña, most delicate
of God's creatures, turning as one
in that ancient silence
to watch us . . . or bless us . . .
Pat's L.A. to New York bus saga
bringing it back to me here
in this other life in the States
where the Greyhounds
humming over the freeways
are disinfected with lysol at night
till they're perfectly spotless,
& sport their own little toilets
& interchangeable drivers
& the American Dream is made manifest—
to be blown in the back seat
by a showgirl from Reno
while racing into the winking,
libidinous eye of that fabulous city
—the one we've been heading out for
all of our lives,
that spasm of throbbing lights
in the unapproachable distance,
luring us on.

IN LIEU OF A LOVE POEM FOR AMERICA

Yesterday an earthquake shook the emerald coast
of Ecuador where years ago,
expatriated by the war, we used to watch
those coconut-umbrella rafts
float down the Rio Esmeraldas,
that fishing port where all the shoeshine boys
would wait outside the restaurants
for us to leave
so they could gobble down our leftovers.
& this, buried on the back pages: some
guy confessed the L.A. cops had paid him
to assassinate George Jackson,
the black revolutionary con they'd gunned down in the yard.
That one stuck in my head a while, too.
Then, in the afternoon, the newest girlfriend
of my neighbor, Eddie, started groaning
on the other side of the dividing wall
while I was reading snatches
out of Bill Wantling's *San Quentin's Stranger*.
All of which I guess is why towards evening,
driving along Mission Bay,
when Sarai suggested that for tomorrow's reading
I compose a quietly effective love poem for America,
it swept over me again— that violent, incapacitating rage.
I didn't say anything of course,
just watched the sunset bleeding over the horizon.
It was absolutely gorgeous
& no less gorgeous for the fact
that three hundred feet above the waters of the bay
a navy chopper twisted in the twilight
like a bloated fly
hovering above a pool of blood,
the spinning halo of its iron blades
buzzing in the dusk.

HARPER'S FERRY

I made a pilgrimage to Harper's Ferry
where that band of revolutionary
Abolitionists was caught.
If the plan had worked
there would have been a black
guerrilla army in the Alleghenies.
The government's rebuilt the arsenal
that Brown was after
& the engine house
where he & his boys
holed up
& held them off.
The old man's still there,
in wax, in the museum,
dressed all in black,
with blazing eyes,
kneeling in a window with his fist
about the barrel of a carbine,
waiting . . .
Harper's Ferry
rises from the Shenandoah
& Potomac rivers
like a rock fortress
& the waters
crash against
the shore
& pound out *freedom . . . freedom . . .*
& the mountains echo back *John*
Copeland. Osawatomie Brown.
Dangerfield Newby. Will Leeman.
Jere Anderson.
     Shields Green. . . .

GUESTS OF THE NATION

We enter in festive spirits
giggling in the dark
amid a handful of indifferent drunks
& empty chairs. The Jolly Trolley,
Christmas Eve. Up front,
two ex-Saigon hookers in stiletto heels,
their bloated breasts
bouncing as they stumble
drunkenly about the stage
are fondling themselves & grinning
for the folks who poured the kerosene
& tossed the match, & then,
astonished at the conflagration,
offered up asylum
to the unincinerated.
Obliviously drunk
& unapproachably tricked out
in that lubricious music,
whirling in a parody of lust,
they seem, if anything,
less naked than the rest of us,
while in the semi-dark
their huge inflated tits
bear witness to,
if not our generosity,
our genius for display & packaging
& the technology of mutilation:
sliced apart, they have been stuffed
like pillows,
or like hunting trophies—
even in this smokey darkness
you can see the scars.
& then it's over. The vocalist
winds back into a sexy whisper
& the saxophone behind her
sputters like a candle
& blows out.

& in that silence,
stripped of the bravado of the dance,
how shyly they bow to us,
how awkwardly,
& are at last
naked & vulnerable.
There is a trickle of applause.
A slot machine in the casino lobby
vomits up its nickels
& as in a seamless dream
of unaccountable transitions
they are back among us
in their blouses & black g-strings
grinning sleepily
& hustling drinks
& dumping out the ashtrays:
nothing much, but it's a living—
Christmas Eve, Las Vegas, 1979.
The end of a decade.

EQUIVOCAL ELEGY

a couple of days ago, out of the blue,
an elderly woman I hardly knew, a stranger,
mentioned the name of a man
who had been a teacher of mine twenty years back
when I was a student at Brooklyn College—
Bernard Grebanier.
A concert pianist & Shakespeare scholar,
he had published two or three
slender volumes of elegant verse— poems
by now, I suppose, long forgotten.
& something, too, of a fool.
A fat, ridiculous goose stuffed with opinions,
he had been one of those
who had borne witness
back in the awful anti-communist purge
of the 50s.
Lives of colleagues,
better men than himself,
had shattered about him like delicate china.
There were those who, even years later,
would turn away when he entered a room.
Yet the man was a splendid teacher.
I had written my first play under his guidance
& learned from him what I know
of the nature of plot
& dramatic action.
Once, I recall, on the subway
into Manhattan,
after I'd tempered praise
of a play of his own
with a slighting remark,
he'd replied in a pique:
"Now listen Steven: if you are going to speak well
of a man for heaven's sake
simply speak well of him!"

& he'd puffed himself up
with one of those little explosive guffaws
as if he were Samuel Johnson or Wilde
& every *bon mot* was immortal.
Just then, I remember, the IRT
had squealed & gone dark as we entered a tunnel.
How vivid it is!
& how grieved I was to hear he had died,
old & alone—
grief, I suppose, in part
for my own past.
The rest of the day
I walked about in the streets
my head swimming with apparitions.
It was the day of the kite festival
here in O.B.
Over my head there were hundreds,
all trembling, adrift
in the clouds—
marvelous, colorful things—
yet for that nothing but delicate tissue,
stretched on the most fragile of ribs,
& held to the wind by a thread.

CONQUISTADOR

While the people looked on from a distance
the President flanked by his aides
stood at the site of the smoldering rubble
where formerly cities had stood.
Shells cratered the fields that remained.
Water, bursting thru shattered dikes,
gushed from a thousand wounds
so that much of what once was the land
was a river, & the river was blood.
All about lay the dead.
"We came in the name of Peace,"
the President cried,
"& the peace has been won!"
Nothing stirred
but the smoke of dead cities
& bubbling mud.
The President opened his fly,
winked at his aides,
& peed
on the bloated corpse of an infant
that lay in the mud.
The populace, somewhat dismayed,
pretended not to have seen,
but that night at the victory feast,
after his toast,
a bird,
the color of ashes,
flew out of the President's egg,
& the diplomats looked at their plates
& nobody said a word.

FRAGMENT OF ANCIENT SKULL

A young man, told to die for his country,
politely declines,
preferring, he mutters, to suck his toes
in his own room.
The civil guard, delighted to practice,
take him outside & shoot him.
His hat blows over the wall.
A piece of his head is found in the brush
centuries later
by entomologists looking for beetles.
Scrubbed down at the local museum
it is stuffed in a jar & labeled:
> *fragment of ancient skull*
> *culture unknown*

But not a word about the fate of his calico,
or the anguish of his father,
or the whereabouts of his hat.

4

Home

CROSSING THE RIVER

I am translating a poem by Domingo Alfonso
called *Crossing the River*.
When I lift my head from the page it is night.
I walk thru the rooms aware of the shapes
that loom in the silence.
In the bedroom Mary has fallen asleep.
I stand in the doorway & watch her breathing
& wonder what it will be like
when one of us dies.
In 8 years
we have not been apart for more than a few days.
The cat drops to my feet & sashays past me.
I open the side door. Outside
there is no sound whatsoever. If things
call to each other at this hour of night
I do not hear them. Vega alone
gleams overhead, thousands of light years
off in the region of Lyra.
The great harp is still.

KIND OF A LOVE POEM

Love, this is the cold truth:
there are no centaurs
or druid spirits
or guardian angels.
No tooth fairy, either.
The Baal Shem Tov
is not about to rise from the dead.
Nor is Jesus.
Nor is Houdini.
Maybe the Ancient of Days
is a good egg
like the bible says
but as for the spirit
outlasting the body,
forget it.
Armageddon perhaps,
but the 2nd Coming
is out of the question.
Yet if emotion endures,
then this,
the song of our life together,
pressed in an old book
like a dead rose,
might fall,
hundreds of years from now,
into the hands
of some archivist
cataloguing the dark ages,
who'll be shaken
back by the song
to his own life,
& shivering,
feel the presence
of ancient lovers,

if only
for that one afternoon
centuries after these arms
that wound about each other
are fragments of bone
& our lips dust
& our names forgotten.

POEM FOR MY PARENTS

For Michael & Billie Kowit,
on the occasion of their 50th wedding anniversary

1

One night, back home in Brooklyn
after 15 years,
I sat around with Mary & the folks
going thru the books of their old photos:
pictures of my dad in knickers
in his late teens looking rakish
in a t-shirt & sailor cap,
holding the center pole of a pup tent—
in his early 20s, hitchhiking
to Montreal & drinking from a flask
at the side of a road.
Next to that, a piece of birch bark
that he sent my mother
from that escapade— postmarked Maine,
Sep. 2   7 a.m.   1926. My mother
with a tennis racket, '27,
& smiling from a swimming pool in '28.
They are sitting on the railing of a ship;
my father in a bowtie & knit sweater,
she beside him, a lovely girl of 16,
their arms & feet touching.
They're just kids. They look beautiful,
both of them, the picture's dated
July 4, 1923.
& there's my mother with the Guild Players
in Disraeli & there they are
at Camp Allegro
surrounded half a century ago by friends
who have remained beloved to this day.
& then they're on their honeymoon
skating on a frozen lake
out in the woods of Pennsylvania

in the faded sepia gold of old snapshots—
a series of them
skating on the ice, holding hands,
my father with a pipe by a pine tree,
my mother leaning on the pillar of the house
where they were honeymooning,
hands sunk in her pockets,
her face gleaming, in the last
of that series Mickey, my father,
has his arms around her,
they stand on the frozen lake
the woods behind them
in their black skates & leather jackets,
he holds her to him,
they are radiantly happy
they have just been married; it is December, 1928,
the ancient, black paper edges
of the photo album
as I turn the pages, crumble
like confetti,
& fall like tears.
Beyond the joy & tenderness & passion
of these early snapshots,
that are dated in the upper corners,
but which time has partially erased,
& against the zeitgeist: all fashion,
the grief of history
& the drift of the age,
I honor them for the steady burning of their devotion.
May all of us be blessed by love
as faithful & unswerving.
They have been married 50 years.

2

Dad, one day over 30 years ago
you rigged a small sail
to an old rowboat
& we set off across a lake
high in the Berkshires.
It was the end of summer,
a day in August bathed in stillness.
I was a small boy, you
a strong, quiet man in your 40s.
Now & then small waves
slapped the thick sides under the oarlocks.
Then a wind came up so fast & quietly
we hardly noticed it until it seized us;
the small boat tossed about
bobbing like a cork. I
grabbed the sides, you worked the sail loose
quickly & unleashed it
& we drifted, oarless, far out,
waving our arms & fruitlessly calling out
to the few oblivious
figures on the dock, the sun
glinting ominously off those high waves.
Had it come to that we might have swum
for the other shore. Summers before
you had taught me: one hand
lifting my belly the other pressing
my back— I would kick & kick
holding the rope with both hands
squinting my eyes from the splashing.
Quiet, gentle, efficient, infinitely patient,
I think you are more
healer than teacher.
In those childhood illnesses,
I would wait hours for your figure
to appear out of the shadows of the hallway;
you would enter the room & say "hi, Butch,"
& sit quietly at the edge of the bed,

& it was the same quiet reassurance of your presence
beside me that summer day, bathed in light,
when we were tossed about on the waters together,
which turned what might have become a small boy's panic
into a kind of bliss
that we were stranded
together,
alone, drifting . . .

& 30 years later felt the same bliss
when we swam together in the warm waters
off the coast of Miami. Alone
with you again I had the same experience
of your gentleness,
your quiet grace & strength.
Dad, I think your tolerance
& patience for the world
has been my strength for 40 years.
Odd, how little we have ever spoken to each other
& how absolute the love that has bound us.
The distance of a continent means nothing.
We are still together,
tho older,
a man & his small son
drifting thru a void
that is turbulent & calm by turns—
marvelous beyond words, ineffable
& exquisite: silent
in a world of absolute stillness
on a lake that is infinite.

3

Ma, you stand at the dining room table & unfold
a paper napkin & place it, a white, translucent shawl
over your dark hair. Then you light two candles.
It is Friday evening. Outside the light is fading
from the world over Brooklyn, over East 14th Street,
with the darkness of early winter. As the room surrenders

to that darkness your white hands circle the small flames
of the two candles: they thin & flicker
under your fingers. Then you close your eyes
& recite the *brocha*. I can barely hear you.
An elevated Brighton Local rumbles thru the darkness
over Kelley Park. The shadow of your body
sways almost imperceptibly against the stairs:
How red your cheeks are in the light
of those two candles. Then the sound of the train
disappears & I hear you sobbing— tears
run down your cheeks.
You cover your face with your hands (perhaps
because I am there at your side in the dark room),
but your grief cannot be contained.
Your body trembles.
The candles, that are for the sabbath,
& honor the creation, are also, like the *yertzite*
candle burning in the glass in the kitchen,
for the dead. For your mother, Bertha,
my grandmother, who has recently died.
& as your grieving shadow sways & sobs
the *brocha*, you have become again
that small girl dancing down Second Avenue
more than half a century ago.
You are in a yellow dress, with ruffles,
you are carrying something home, some fish
or fruit wrapped in newspaper a page
from the *Daily Forvitz*, you are dancing
among the pushcarts of Delancey Street,
you are dancing thru the door of the settlement house
& under the impoverished tenement stairways
of the east side.
In this family portrait your father's image
is dissolving as you & your brothers & sisters
blossom into your own lives.
Now you are married, now the chaos
of the great depression, now Mickey graduates
from law school, you give birth to a daughter,
& a son. The pitiless war like an evil wind:

your brothers disappear
for 4 years. They write from the battlefields
of France. There are tormented, desperate phonecalls
in Yiddish. The Jews of Europe are slaughtered.
The screendoor of the apartment in Bensonhurst slams shut.
Roosevelt dies. We move in with your mother in the Bronx;
Rosemont catches fire; you buy the house
on 14th Street; Camp Tamarack & the Pines,
& the black Plymouth & college for the kids
& Carol's wedding. Your son
kisses you goodbye & flies off to California.
It flickers, all of it, on the wall by the stairs
with your weeping shadow twenty years ago.
As I watch you there, in silence, helpless,
not just my mother now, but a woman, swaying
over the sabbath candles in the most ancient grief,
how my heart embraces you,
tho I say nothing. Not a word. How dark it is
& how quiet. We are alone. Dad is dozing in the dark
in the other room. Carol is upstairs with her homework;
the last gray light of the day seeps thru the curtain.
A loaf of challah catches the light. It stands on
a silver tray on a white cloth. The tissue paper shawl
on your dark hair shivers in the flame
& glows with its own light.
& then it is done.
Your hands withdraw from your face.
The *brocha* ends. & the sobbing.
& when you take off that shawl all the past
disappears into those two, small yellow flames.
I wake Dad up, & standing at the foot of the stairs
yell for Carol to come down to dinner
& now you are taking the roast out of the oven & dad
does his funny cakewalk into the dining room,
that mischievous grin on his face & you say,
"Mick, don't be such a wise-guy, please"
& I laugh, & Carol sets the table & I
grab a piece of challah & dad grabs a piece of challah too,
& ma, you tell us to hold our horses & you

complain about having to put the roast back three times
but your face is beaming— your complaint full of joy
& I squeal I have to have gravy, I can't eat
anything without gravy, Carol brings in the potatoes
& we're all talking at once, the mindless
yammer of delight about the feast you have prepared
for us so lovingly— with such devotion—
that you have always prepared for us—
& it's great, ma . . .
it's absolutely delicious— all these years,
the feast you have made for us all. Ma, it's wonderful
it's absolutely wonderful.

—November 1978

THE ROSE

Home late, I eat dinner
& read the paper
without noticing
the rose in the yellow
glass on the dining room table—
not until
Mary shows it to me.
"Isn't it lovely?"
"Where'd you get it?"
"A fellow named Bill."
"Oh?"
"Just some guy who comes in
to the bar occasionally . . .
Isn't it lovely?"
"He gave it to you?"
I turn to the editorial page.
"Yes . . .
he just got out of the hospital."
She bends
& takes in its fragrance.
She is wearing that black negligee.
"The hospital?"
She straightens up & looks
at me & sighs.
"He's dying of cancer."
We stare at each other.
I want to embrace her,
tell her how much I love her,
how much I have always loved her.
But I don't.
I just sit there.
When she walks back into the bedroom
I see it at last,
glowing on the table,
leaning toward me
on its heartbroken stem.

JOY TO THE FISHES

I hiked out to the end of Sunset Cliffs
& climbed the breakwater,
sneakers strung over my shoulder ´
& a small collection of zen
poems in my fist.
A minnow
that had sloshed out of someone's baitbucket,
& that I came within an inch of stepping on,
convulsed in agony.
Delighted to assist,
I tossed it back into its ocean:
swirling eddies sucked about the rocks,
white pythagorean sailboats
in the middle distance.
Kids raced the surf,
a labrador brought down a frisbee,
& the sun sank pendulously
over the Pacific shelf.
I shivered & descended,
slipping the unopened book
into my pocket
& walked south
along the southern California coastline—
all the hills of Ocean Beach
glowing
in the rouged light
of midwinter sunset.
Even now
it pleases me to think
that somewhere
in the western coastal waters off America
that minnow is still swimming.

405

I figured to leave early,
drive the coast road,
score a Chinese restaurant
& lay out by the ocean
for a while
& get stoned & write
& watch the women,
hit the buyers,
spend the afternoon with Bill,
catch the sun
sinking over the Pacific,
& be home for dinner.
But it didn't pan out:
I got off to a late start,
killed an hour in a bookstore,
settled for a jack-in-the-box
bean burrito.
The beach was out,
the buyers weren't in,
the sun went down without me.
Bill & I embraced
& parted
in a single gesture.
Around midnight,
driving back on 405,
it came to me
how quickly
everything was passing,
& suddenly
it was all luminous—
the abacus of lights,
the moon, cold
wind whipping
thru the window
& my self alive,
impermanent . . .

for the eleven millionth time
I vowed to change my life.
A mist came up,
the night settled in about me
& I dreamed sweetly
of all that I will never become—
women, wisdom, poetry & revolution
disappearing
in the purr of the engine
& the moan of the road
& the song of the radio.

LULLABY

—after Atila Josef

Sweet love, everything
closes its eyes now to sleep.
The cat
          has stretched out
at the foot of your bed
& the little bug
                    lays its head
in its arms
& your jacket
that's draped on the chair:
every button has fallen asleep,
even the poor torn cuff...
                    & your flute
& your paper boat
& the candy bar
                    snug in its wrapper.
Outside,
the evening is closing its eyes.
Even the hill to the dark
woods
has fallen asleep
on its side
          in a quilt of blue snow.

RAKING IN

            I pull into the driveway.
Mary, in a bright red bandana,
is raking the leaves.
When I left this morning
grosbeaks & chickadees
sat in the feeder but
now nothing sings but the leaves:
                life is precious
                precious
                        the dead leaves sing.

I take up the other rake & join in.

These are the leaves
that have lain all winter
under the snow.
They are sodden & faded.
I am careful to rake in
only the dead,
leaving the lovely wild
plum & yellow crocuses
standing—
the first of our flowers to bloom.

Simply that: we are together
raking the lawn,
                life is ended too soon
                too soon
                        the dead leaves sing.

THE DEAD MAGICIAN

They surround me on the beach as well they should.
I am the drowned man, now worthy of what I suffered,
awesomely still, surrounded by approval
& terror. Eternal now, but for me
the sky could not be this blue,
nor the lone, low, predatory buzzard
gliding above the sea,
so black,
so deliberately beautiful.
Years later they'll recall a day in summer
when the whole of reality trembled like the white
sheet they covered me with,
thinking to mute my power.
A shoe full of small change,
a wallet & watch under a towel
wrapped in a shirt up the beach—
such was my life, such are the attributes
I have been emptied of.
The usual things. Dying
was one of the few occasions
that shook me out of my slumber.
They hauled me ashore— in death
a hideous fishlike creature,
much the sort that will surface up in one's dreams:
the head of a mythological beast—
grotesque, inhumanly bloated,
but almost familiar—
bobbing up out of the deep & then being sucked under.

OUT OF McHENRY

Broken fence thru the mist.
Bitter fruit of the wild pear
& vines full of berries.
The stone path
buried in brambles
& mud
& the shack in ruins,
rotted thru
like an old crate:
half the roof caved in.
The whole place
gone to weed & debris.
Someone before me
sick of his life
must have figured this
was as far away as he'd get
& nailed it up
out in the void
then died here
or left
decades ago.
A swallow
skitters among the beams
& flies out
thru the open frame of a window.
Now nothing inhabits the place
but tin cans
covered with webs,
a mattress,
a handful of tools
busted & useless —
& myself
where he stood
here in the doorway,
in mist,
high up over this world.
Trees & flowers dripping with cold rain.

THE PRIZE

Solemn proceedings or not, when they
bellowed my name out over the mike
I leaped to my feet
like a Yankee fan on a long fly:
"Yahoo— that's me!" I screamed out
waving my hat in the air.
It was my name alright
although oddly pronounced
& all but drowned out by applause.
Here & there I could see the gentility
wriggle & stiffen, rolling their eyes.
Not that I cared. I mean really,
how could they blame me— I
who'd been chosen. "Please,
please excuse me," I laughed,
pushing my way thru the millions.
The first waves obligingly parted.
I think someone even slapped me
joyfully on the back,
tho perhaps not, perhaps
it was simply the mass of humanity
surging forward & back.
& why had they chosen me? Frankly,
tho I had been waiting for just such a moment
my whole life
I hadn't the faintest idea.
Others, not I after all, had invented the drum
& the stone axe & the digital clock,
had been first to domesticate corn,
had turned north at the Solomon Islands,
had defeated the Scourge of God at Chalons,
taken that first leap with a parachute
over the Balkans, dreamed up
the collapsible cup & the folding chair
& the wave goodbye & the kiss
with the mouth open.

Someone else had scaled Annapurna,
walked on the moon,
broken the codes of the double helix & linear B.
My own accomplishments had been, if not modest,
at best known to no more
than an intimate circle of friends.
Still & all, I had been chosen
& certainly not without reason.
However, with every step closer I got
to what I assumed was the front of the great hall,
the more difficult it became
to press my way thru
the opaque, intransigent flesh
of my fellow creatures.
Now & again, on my toes, over their shoulders,
I managed to glimpse what I supposed
was the stage, tho vastly further away
than one would have guessed— a blue light
shimmering up at the dais,
the lectern in front with its glass of cold water,
the chap with the mustache & cummerbund
holding in one hand the slip with my name
& coughing uneasily into the other.
"Hold on, I'm coming!"
I yelled into that tunnel of enormous backs.
But could anyone hear me?
& how long would they wait?
How long would they hold up whatever it was
that came next? Surely the time would approach
when they'd simply proceed as if I had never existed.
Tho I am not complaining, believe me.
They have been patient this long, these many years,
the crowd hasn't thinned in the slightest,
the mc is waiting there yet, the paper
flapping about at the tips of his fingers
while I fight my way thru to the spotlight
where I belong, as painfully as a man
trying to run underwater.

84

"Hold on . . . I'm coming!" I cry out,
hoarse with expectation & anguish— older,
older by decades,
& all but exhausted now,
but not a whit diminished in spirit— no,
not in the least. Slower perhaps
& for that a trifle more desperate,
but still, in this roiling human sea,
the aging grin on my face
as buoyant & simple & open as a canoe—
still unrelentingly optimistic,
confident to a fault,
enthusiastic as ever,
despite everything, downright ebullient:
"Hold on . . . hold on. I'm coming . . . I'll be right there!"

LAST WILL

If I am ever
unlucky enough to die
(God forbid!)
I would like to be propped up
in my orange overstuffed chair
with my legs crossed
dressed in a cashmere sweater
& jeans
& embalmed
in a permanent glaze
like a donut
or Lenin
a small bronze plaque
on the door of my study
showing the dates
of my incarnation & death.
& leave the room as it was!
Let nothing be touched in the house!
My underpants stuck on the doorknob
just where I left them.
My dental floss
lying on top of the Bhagavad Gita
next to my socks.
Let the whole of Ebers Street
be roped off
& planted with yews
from Narragansett to Cape May
& left as a monument to my passing.
The street?
No— the city itself!
Henceforth
Let it be known
as the Steve M. Kowit
Memorial Park & Museum.
Better yet
if the thing can be done

without too much fuss
put the whole planet to sleep.
Let the pigeons & busses
& lawyers & ladies
hanging out wash
freeze in their tracks.
Let the whole thing
be preserved under ice
just as it looked
when the last bit of drool
trickled over my chin.
Let the last of the galaxies
sizzle out
like a match in the wind
& the cosmic balloon
shrink down to a noodle
& screech to a halt.
Let time clot
like a pinprick of blood
& the great solar flame
flicker down
to the size of a *yertzite* candle
leaving the universe dark
but for one tiny spotlight
trained on the figure of me
propped in my chair—
for after my death
what possible reason could life
in any form
care to exist?
—Don't you see
it would be utterly pointless!
I would be gone!
Look, try to conceive it,
a world without *me*! Me
entirely absent—
nobody here with these eyes,
this name,
these teeth!

Nothing but vacant space
a dry sucking wind
where I walked
where I sat— where
you used to see me
you would see nothing at all—
I tell you
it dwarfs the imagination ...
Oh yes, one last thing:
the right leg
is to be crossed over the left
— I prefer it that way —
& poised on the knee
prop the left elbow up
on the arm of the chair
with a pen
in my right hand—
let my left
be characteristically
scratching my skull
or pulling my hair.
If you wish
close the lids of my eyes
but whatever you do
the mouth must remain open
just as it was in life—
yes
open forever!
On that I absolutely insist!

CODICIL

Look, if it can't be arranged
then forget it.
But make certain
I have a clean shave, okay?
& my nails aren't filthy
& my poor dead nose
doesn't dribble over my shirt
during the service.
& if you could
put a nice clean pillow
under my head
in the casket—
I know it sounds silly
but I could never
sleep soundly without one—
preferably soft
but if it comes to that
any old pillow will do.
& please, no cut flowers:
just let the weeds of the place
be permitted to flourish
over the stone. Alive,
they are lovely enough
in their own right.
& friends
how pleased I would be
if you sniffled a bit
when they lower me
into the ground
& if, even years later,
you still think of me
now & again— if nothing
more than one of my gestures
or jokes— or better yet
a figure from one of my poems
that had always stuck in your head

nudging open the heart
with its grace
or disarming humor—
a moment
in which the world
is made new
& mysterious
& I am alive
& we are together again.

LI HO

Battling the fierce wind of the northern frontier
I dismount
clutching my satchel of verse
& a gourd of wine
they sold me on credit.
Weeds shiver. White water
thunders into its gorge.
Lichen seeps over the rock.
My poor mare whinnies with cold.
At every step
leaves torn by the wind
swarm at my ankles, like gnats,
& crumble under my feet
like small bones.
Ghosts?
or only the rolling mist of the Gobi
moaning among the disconsolate hills?
& I— if I seem to have disappeared
in this vast white scroll
it is just that at 20,
my hair is already as white
as the damp shroud of the northern slope.
Look closely!
I am that speck of ink
in the wash of dissolving hills
at the interface of the visible world
& the void—
that stroke of light in the mist.

DUSK IN THE CUYAMACAS

It was that tangerine
& golden
sepia light
spilling over the Cuyamacas
—each leaf
of the manzanita
chiselled in space—
that shook me out of my dreams
till I woke again
to my own life:
everything shimmering
everything just as it is.

HOME

You arrive in Paradise feverish with anticipation, assuring yourself that everything will be perfect — no migraine head-aches, no ambulance sirens, no goodbyes. & it's true, the view from your sitting room is breathtaking, the service impecca-ble, the food enticingly garnished, & although the water tastes slightly metallic, there is always the coke machine in the lobby. & the climate — the sort of weather you love, one glorious day on the heels of another. You stroll down the beach under the mangroves & seagrape trees in love, as you were on Earth, with the word *oceano*, white seagulls, the bronzed & half-naked women — women who are everything you have always dreamed, & yours for the taking. Truly a lecher's heaven. Yes, everything's perfect, perfect by definition . . . till one afternoon in an unguarded mood you confess to yourself that the cuisine is without flavor & the wine flat, that the celestial muzak piped into your suite, however mellifluous, jangles your nerves. How you wish you could turn on the radio & hear Monk or Dylan or even the six o'clock news. You long, if the truth be known, for a cup of cold water. As for the women, however lovely to look at, to the touch they are as lifeless as the pages of the magazines from which they were drawn, & as weightless & predictable as the figments of your own imagination.

It is just then —at that very instant— that the thread of a name & face catches the light on what remains of the delicate film of your cortex, the wraith of a memory . . . & escapes. You call to it desperately over & over, but it will not return, tho its residue lingers on your tongue. Such is the other side of God's marvel-ous amnesia. From that day forward you are lost. You pace in distraction along the Elysian beach obsessed with the need to recall who it was & what it must have been like. How insuffer-able, at such moments, is the glare of Paradise! & so it is that with only your foolish heart for a witness, you begin to long bitterly for home.